Contents

Enjoy, the, Book,

Bill, Booth, JNR,

In Reach of St. Polycarp's

This book is in memory our brother John. Without him, Alan and Ray, this book would not be possible. GOD BLESS HIM.

Special thanks to Joan Malone who patiently sifted through my bad handwriting and managed to set out the book in a comprehensible order.

THANK YOU, JOAN,

River Mersey

The river stands majestic
Surrounded on all sides
By history and its buildings
By ships that have passed by

Yet you trundle on forever
Amidst the changing sky
The river has been our livelihood
It graced a thousand years
It's carried souls to far off lands
Amidst their hopes and fears
It's always been a lady too
So gentle in its ways
From King John's words
Its lasted all these days

The river takes its daily toll
And grades all that's new
It ebbs its way through history
Without a bling or two
It's always been there for us
The passion and the fear
The river it remains sublime
In every passing year

She will always be in our blood
As the waves bombard the quay
But all our wealth rests on this soul
That is the River Mersey

W.H. Booth Jnr (Billy Booth)

Preface

This story is recorded around the time when children could play safely in the street without having to worry who they were playing with or who they were talking to. When parents joined in street games with children and when the men would play football in the streets with kids on their way back from the pub. When boys were boisterous and girls played girl games like hopscotch. Innocent times in the 1950's and 1960's when times and people seemed safer. When everyone was in the same boat and no cars in the street, no-one trying to be what they are not. They all pulled together as neighbours, all with the same goal in life; to bring up their families the best way they could.

The names and places in this book are all fact, nothing is left out. This is based on a family brought up in and around Great Homer Street/ Netherfield Road/Scotland Road. Their day to day life, their school days, their leisure days and their working days, all set in a salt of the earth area of Everton, Liverpool 5.

Chapter one

40 Gordon Street – Family and Friends

We as a family were brought up in 40 Gordon Street, in the borough of Everton, off Great Homer Street and Netherfield Road. The two major landmarks were St Georges Church, Everton Road and St. Anthony's Church, Scotland Road. Sandwiched in the middle was the Protestant Church of St Polycarp's at the top of Conway Street.

We were a family of eight, mam, dad and six kids. There were five boys and one girl who came last in line. My man and dad were determined to have a girl and eventually it happened. The four eldest boys will figure mostly in this book purely because there was only one year between each of us and we worked better as a team than individually although we all had our talents which will feature later on in the book.

Our names, starting with me the eldest, are William (Billy), John, Alan and Ray. Nine years later came Wayne and twelve months after Wayne was Gail. Now with the family complete the story begins.

We came from very humble beginnings living at the above address. My dad worked as a docker and my mother somehow has the time to work as a cleaner from 5am, returning home at 8am to get us kids off to school, only to return to work at 5pm, returning home at 8:30pm and carry on with any housework and make sure we were all asleep before she and dad could have their tea together before they went to bed. Ready for the same routine the next day.

The house was a two up, two down terrace, back to back type with an entry at the back. Separating both back to back backyards there were as many as 40 houses on each side of the street separated only by an oller and side streets which housed the Gordon Arms Public House and bang in the middle of the street on one side was Maggie Blakes Sweets and General Store next to the oller (short for a waste ground or bombed out site).

My mam and dad spent many a good night in the Gordon Arms. Maggie Blake was mostly responsible for the funds or entrance fee if you like into the pub. You could borrow from her on a Monday and pay it back on the Friday only to repeat the process the following week. Although there were many money lenders both Maggie and her husband had a heart of gold and the shop never seemed to close, open all hours to coin a phrase. We would often get sweets for nothing, they were great. She would sell lose ciggies, toffee apples, ice lollies, twicers, sticky lice, walkers, caramels, mojo's, black jacks and every sweet that captivated our early years. As young lads and girls, finding the money to fund such delights will keep you amused and shocked through this journey.

As it was a close-knit community everyone born in Liverpool 5 was down to earth, salt of the earth, I have heard it said they were proud and very hard-working people and would have nothing said of the area they lived in or of their neighbours and their friends. Everyone was in the same boat, both financially and domestically; no-one had any money to talk of. They lived form Monday to Friday and went about their business, proud in the fact that they had clothed and fed and brought up their children in the best way they could.

27-29 Gordon Street, off Netherfield Road

Greaty was a jewel in the crown when it came to shops. A haven of choice in shops, pubs, picture houses and schools and of course hand carts or better known as barrows. Ladies, let's start with the shops, all famous names – Melias, Sturlas, Gordons, Reeces, Woolworths, Levers and Martins and Whites cake shop, Duffys, Chandlers, Charles the Taylors, Jacksons barbers, Walter Woods butchers, Leos Ice-cream shop, Stephenson's chippy, Savas chippy, Fred's Wallpaper and Paints, Ronnie Follit and Joe Bristow's fruit and veg shops, Thomo's fruit and veg shop, Aughtersons tea shop, Marys pork shop, Freeman Hardy and Willis shoe shop, Duttons sweet shop, O'Niels bicycle shop, the famous Schofieds lemonade factory off Darlymple Street, Greenburgs, the famous glass people, the list goes on. An Aladdin's cave of shops open from dawn 'til dusk, where you could buy anything, and not forgetting the most used shop in Greaty. I have won a fortune asking people from Greaty, do you remember this shop? Not many knew it. Of-course, it was the famous spot, you could buy anything in there from a needle to a baby elephant... and all made in Hong Kong little acorns hey!

Then there were the pubs down Greaty. There were bents pubs, Bass houses, Threlfall's, Walkers, Cains, Tetley's etc. When I had my first pint as a 15-year-old it was in one of these pubs. The Brown Cow, just off Cazeneu Street. Also, the Myrtle Arms in Boundary Street, which was my other choice at that age to sample a brown over bitter, no lager in those days. Anyway, on with our pub crawl. We had the Conway castle and the Grapes, the Aporto, the Edinburgh, the clock, the Bents House at the bottom of Bossy, ie Bostock Street.

Then we have the picture houses. There was the Popular, affectionately known as the Pop, we had the Rossi, and the Gaity, the Jem, the Derby and of course, the famous Rotunda Theatre, just before my time. But the Homer in Greaty, known locally as the bug house, was our local picture house. It was at the very heart of Greaty, it really had a heartbeat and the commissioner was a very good friend of my granddad. I later was told his name was Paddy Donnelly; he was an institution in those days. He was kitted out in his uniform, full epaulette's, he was a big man; you never got passed him, never. He would stand at the top of the steps and say, "you're not 16, you can't come in". So off we went to find someone to take us in as their son, it always worked. When we got in it was great.

Sweets would come flying from everywhere, bad tomatoes, oranges and grapes, fade apples the lot. The Saturday matinee was something else. It was what we looked forward to all week and where we spent that money, we had earned form all of our exploits during the week, which we will come to later.

The churches really stood for something in those days. Whether you were catholic or protestant, the churches were a powerful force and the priests and reverends were revered and respected and no-one crossed them. They were held in great esteem. Both churches had power. St Anthony's of Scotland road and St Polycarp's off Netherfield road, the church where we spent our Saturday afternoons, or at least we should have. We were either playing on the tarmac or in Otterspool with our dad.

Before my dad worked on the dock, he would do ship scaling, a very dirty job, that entailed cleaning out the ships' tanks of dirty oil. He would work overnight. He would be filthy and full of oil when he came in. As dock work was casual, times were very hard for my parents with six kids to feed. When no work was available, my dad would rent a handcart, a barrow, from Paki, short for Packenham, the local scrap metal dealers. He would collect scrap, iron, rags, metals etc down back entries. He would do anything to feed his family. He was a very proud man and he would rather push a hand cart round the streets than stand outside a pub and bum and cadge a drink off anyone. Our dad was a grafter. He was very crafty, he had a quick brain. He could add anything up in his head, no calculator for him. He was gifted, as well as his quick brain he had an uncanny knack of making money. Wherever he went he was in great demand. He was a great darts player. He was called the man with the golden arm. Two of my brothers took after him. Our john and Wayne.

They were as good as him although they all thought they were the best. He was always winning trophies. His greatest asset was his voice, he had the best around and he had the most beautiful sweet voice, that of an angel for sure. Along with his dark good looks he would charm the birds from the trees. So, you could imagine those days of no telly and no stay behinds in pubs, how popular he was, not so though with our mam. The Elizabeth Taylor lookalike, she was beautiful. She had to stay at home with the six kids whilst my dad was out, if not playing darts he would be entertaining at someone's house party along with a few crates of Guinness or brown ale.

The house nearly always had a piano, if not, so what, guess who was the star turn? It was my dad. He was very popular and had loads of mates and if anyone played the squeeze box or piano in the pub, he would be up singing. He was a real showman, sadly no-one takes after him with his voice, although my sister Gail would have given him a run for his money, she's that good!

Great Homer Street

I feel the entire lads have inherited my dad's other talents which were his zest for life, his energy, his eye for a bargain, even though it was sold on again when he was off with the barrow. He would be out in all weathers, uphill and down dale, mostly uphill because Everton was the highest point in Liverpool and the streets here steep, to name a few Fairy street, Havelock Street and Mittford street. He would mostly weigh in, a term used in scrap yards, scrap metal, light iron, rags, maybe a bit of shinning gold that is copper or brass if he was lucky. He may have picked up some antiques while shouting up the entries "scrap iron, scrap iron and any old scrap iron". The antiques and bric-a-brac he would sell on to an antique shop on Scotland Road or indeed pawn, never to redeem. He was a crafty bucker and a hard act to follow. Though we all loved him, as kids we never knew until we got older how he made a living. He would often have people inform the benefits department because he was always doing something with his day, rather than bumming pints outside a pub; he was not lazy like the others. Remember he had six kids to support, my dad was proud, he didn't have a lazy bone in his body. You would never find him doing what some do today, watching day time telly. I was proud of him then and we are proud of him now! We often had kids calling after us like "your dads a rag man, your dads a tatter, are them clothes you're wearing yours or someone else's, do them shoes fit or are they fitted with cardboard inside"? but like my dad we were proud so one day they would eat their words, it will come. Later it is called poetic justice. Our mother was the backbone of the family, an Elizabeth Taylor double. Everyone said she was beautiful and she was. She loved my dad and idolised her kids. We were all the apple of her eye! She worked seven days a week for us with no comforts at all. She had some energy our mam. She would leave the house early and have to go back out again at tea time, arriving home at 8pm. Once home she would carry on at home. At night, after our tea we would play out under the lamp outside our house, then she or my dad would call us in and it was off to bed, n mistake, she was hard but fair. She would argue with anyone in the street to protect us lads. Like all kids, we were up to all kinds, but nothing illegal. If anyone knocked, she would say "what have they done now"? are you sure it was my lads? She was scared of no-one. She was well like in the street and we were always well dressed. We had new clothes on bank holidays and Sunday best. My dad would come back from the pub on a Sunday and take us to Otterspool on the No 20 bus. We would play football whilst my dad slept off the ale. Wed pick blackberries and roll down the hill, then we'd make dad go for an ice-cream each. Back on the bus home for Sunday tea, ice cream, cakes and jellies that's what you call Sundays.

Mum and Dad – Elizabeth Taylor & Dean Martin

Also a great part of our life was our nan Kate, who also lived at 40 Gordon Street, before moving to Eastbourne Street off Everton Brow. She was amazing. Less than 5ft tall, 15-16 stone and was stronger than an ox. She had 7 children, four girls and 3 lads.

Our mother was one her daughters. My granddad was in the navy and died very young. We never knew him which was a real shame, from the stories my nan told. He was a seaman and I was a seaman. What tales he would have told us kids. He died of pneumonia back in the 1930's it was common then. My nan was proud like me mam.

All the kids were well behaved and disciplined and what a struggle it must have been to feed seven kids. My granddad was only 38 when he died, my aunties and uncles very young at the time, must have been devastated. I know my nan was.

My nan worked hard to feed her kids, she sold flowers, she sold fish and she sold door to door carrying her youngest child with her. My nan and

I were very close. I was her first grandchild when she would have been around 50. She would visit all her grandchildren. She was a great help to my mam and no one argued with her and like my mam she did not scare easily.

My nan also ran a big house in Eastbourne street that took in Irish navvies and families. My nan lived in the back room whilst four families occupied the rest of the house. She was kept busy keeping the navvies, sometimes drunk, in order. She had plenty of family and friends and never bothered with another man. After granddad, I would often stay the night. I was never able to get in or out of the bed because it was big and I was little then. I used to have porridge and camp coffee or chicory it was called, I love that smell. I was spoilt and then back home to our own bed. Four of us sleeping together in a single, two up one end and two down the other. I will never forget her, she died in 1993 aged 96. What a woman. At the time of her death she had 100 grandchildren from grand to grand to great to great to great. We all thought she would have lived to 100. But she didn't.

Nan and Mam – two peas in a pod

Dad and Gail's daughter, Clare – November 30

Chapter Two

Four young entrepreneurs

We were all very well respected as a family and as four young boys, we were into everything and our exploits and pursuits to make money will amuse you. We never gave our parents any problems and never brought trouble to the door. It was only one time a policeman came to the door but that will come later, I asked my mother when she was ill did we ever cause you any trouble, were we ever a burden. Her answer was "I laughed more than I cried". Those few words meant a lot. We as four likely lads always tried to work the ORACLE and with our choir boy faces and bright blue eyes, we all made good actors and mostly got away with things. We would give and take and take and give, and give mostly to our parents who I am sure were grateful for the extra cash. People depended on us. We had a lot of outlets, from Pakis scrap metal dealers to Sava's and Johns chip shop and all the handcart ladies selling clothes on Greaty market and for the farmers on the market we would load and unload their wagons promptly. Our Alan also found time after doing his 5:30am paper round with our John to deliver milk with the milkman, all before school. From then on the real work begins and the challenge of another day looms to make money. It was a haven of opportunities, if you could work and we could, from 5:00am to 9pm summer and winter. We could coin it in none of us were lazy. We all had a role and we played it to perfection. Great Homer street and Netherfield road just opened up. If we had it, we could sell it. Nothing was sacred. Even sewer and gutted grids! We would pinch them and the off to Aladdin's cave that is 40 Gordon Street, tradesman's entrance. For a space of about 10ft x 6ft if you wanted anything, we had it and if it wasn't the right colour, we painted it. There were slates, lead, copper, wire, brass, handles, letter boxes, toilet seats and doors. Toilet seats were our favourites, real money to be made there. There were mirrors, windows, window sashes, sash weights, bricks, tiles, tea chests, aluminium, you name it, we would get it, if not me, then Alan or John. At this point in our business we were beginning to introduce Ray in to the fold, we all had a purpose which we filled down to the letter.

Our days would begin on the way to school after our morning jobs. We would all go by the way of the entries. We would look for rags, steri milk bottles, jam jars, beer bottles, metals, prams and wood. We would lift the metal bins off the wall, each one weighing half a hundred weight. We were all string and each bin had something. All of our goods were stored in one of the bombed-out houses for later that day. Anything of real value went straight back to 40 Gordon street, waiting to be sorted at dinner time. We would then start collecting wood for our night time, full time pursuit of selling firewood. This was a real earner and was not just a part time pursuit. This was serious!

During the week and especially during the school holidays if we were not playing football and it was our greatest passion, we would be searching the entries walking along the back-yard walls seeing if there was anything worth removing. Toilet seats were the real money earners. With them all being wood they were all the same. We would pinch them, paint them and sell them on, mostly to the people we stole them off. They were none the wiser. We would call that night with the firewood, ask them if they wanted any messages or anything the y wanted to get rid of like old newspapers, which we collected. If they said someone had nicked the toilet seat, we said we would look for one in the bombed-out houses. We would return the next day. It would be a shilling for the firewood and two shillings and sixpence, half a crown, for the toilet seat and if you need anything else sir, just ask, and sir could you please carry on saving the newspapers, jam jars, milk bottles, beer bottles? Thank you and bye!

Everton Brow next to Eastbourne Street where my nan lives

The bombdi (the bombed-out houses) were real gems when it came to making money. We were lucky because not only did we have to do these things for treats, like sweet money, Xmas club money and Easter club money but to help mam and dad. Most other families did not have four kids, mostly two, some only one, so they never had a need to do what we did. Both parents had good jobs so other kids thought it was beneath them. Not us! We excelled. It was an endeavour for us inspirational, entrepreneurial, all the things were for us, four young kids aged 8,9,10 & 11. We were so young! We were all clued up and ahead of the rest. Anyone who needed the money, and there were hundreds in this area who were really poor but not with the zest or energy or enthusiasm that we put in to it. We never tired, winter or summer. People relied on the Booths for their goods and they got them.

We had a few bad days when we were kids when my brother Alan got rheumatic fever. We were all worried. My mam and dad were really upset but it got over it. He was as string as an ox. There were days when my mam was running back and forth to Stanley Hospital, one of us would have fallen off a back-yard wall in to an entry or fallen into the cellar of an empty house. The later happened one day when we were all in a house by the oller in Conway Street, facing Chris's shop whilst lifting the copper wire running through the ceiling space when our ray was screaming 'help, its dark and I'm cut to pieces'. We eventually found him. But this accident was eventually a god send. Not only did Ray land on sacks of coins, but they had broken his fall and it could have been a lot worse for him. Me, Alan and John started to open the sacks. A virtual treasure chest. There were three penny bits, tanners, shillings, two bob pieces, half corns. It was great! We had struck gold! This lot never went back to 40 Gordon Street. We moved the bags, left our ray there, planted the bags elsewhere and then took Ray home. My mam was hysterical and we prayed ray would keep quiet. That was difficult with ray because out of the four of us, he was a grass. With the loot moved on, we were set for a massive share out. This we did over the years. Calculating what we took from our daily exploits, this money was carefully added to my mam's weekly income from us. We knew how the money got there. We knew who it belonged to, but no-one knew we had it … only the four of us.

The money belonged to a local bookie who had a stand or pitch if you like on the oller next to Robart Court. Everyone put their bets on with him at the Gordon Arms and the Threllies. He was there day in and day out and that is where he put his cash. But he never gambled on the Booths being in that cellar. We kept it to ourselves and we lived to tell the tale.

Gordon Arms and Crisses shop McGill Street

On Saturdays we would make out way to Paki's scrap yard at the bottom of the entry, to weigh in our weekly hoard after borrowing a barrow from him. We would start moving the metal, brass, copper etc. that was the real McCoy. Then the aluminium, scrap iron, rags and then finally jam jars. We were getting paid £2-£4 on Saturday mornings, which was a lot of money in those days in the 1950's, when my dad was only earning £8 a week. We were not doing badly when this was put with our door to door paper collection which sold on to the local chip shop. Ties from our Rays collection, those robbed from washing lines or those found in bins would be washed, ironed and sold on to local market traders. Shirts, trousers, waist coats, all cleaned and sold on in the same way and not forgetting our main source of income, selling firewood, which will come later. We were not doing badly and my mam was well looked after in every way, both in income and new household goods. My mother was house proud and we turned up nearly every penny that we earned, not all mind, we were not that soft. We would call up to Lizzie Moses shop and out of our wood money we would put a shilling a week in her Xmas club, 3p or sixpence a week in to her Easter egg club. It was a great feeling at Xmas going along with my mam to Lizzies on the corner of the entry in Elias Street and picking up boxes on Xmas Eve with me mam when everyone was in bed. Then putting the goods in my dad's socks with nuts, tangerines, apples and then on the bed posts for John, Alan, and Ray. The other two Wayne and Gail were only babies. It used to give me great pride and a fresh sense of achievement knowing we had helped in our own way to help our mam and dad get by, as well as seeing others faces. They were great days!

The four brothers – Alan, Bill, Ray and Wayne – sadly no John (deceased 1999)

Pakis scrapyard – Packenhams, Gordon Street

Our whole purpose in life was to explore and prosper. We were streets ahead of the other kids. We ran the football, we ran the games. Everyone wanted to be with us. On Saturday Alan and John would go to the market at 6:00am to help the farmers and most of the time they would be paid in fruit and veg, which was a great help. I would carry oil cloth or lino as it's called today to wherever they lived; I got about a shilling for that. Anything we made on a Saturday, we kept and spent it in the Horner picture house. We would go to my nanas on a Sunday or play football on the tarmac or on Neddy, no business on Sundays in those days. No-one worked on Sundays, it was Gods day. Roll on Monday and it would all start over again, we loved a challenge.

I along with a mate George Maddox, used to do a bet on the horses only sixpence (2.5p) taken from our stash of cash. One day we won after giving some man our ticket to collect. We had £38 between us. Each day we would have a bet. Maybe a tanner or so. We planted the money in a bombed-out house in Aughton Street. We went to it every day for months, then one day we went it the bloody house had been demolished! That's what you get for being tight, poetic justice. Obviously, me and George fell out over that but who cares about that now. There was always another scam around the corner.

As we came out of the summer months, approaching the winter, every street and gang were saving the wood for the bomi night on the 5th of November, obviously we didn't. we needed to sell it and we would sometimes raid other people's stashes as the wood became scarce. But bomi night was a real earner for us, not only was loads thrown out on the fires but all of the waste afterwards was there for the taking. You had to be up early next morning, no milkman, no paper delivery, this was serious stuff. Me, Alan and John and now Ray had handcarts, prams steering carts and we would visit as many bomi's as possible before light, or before people stirred. We would rake the fire, the hot metal door handles, brass number plates, aluminium door numbers, copper wire, old prams, shells, lead, light iron, horse shoes, old kettles and pots and pans. This went on for hours and all back to 40 Gordon Street for sorting once it had cooled down. We loved the thrill, the adventure of being one step ahead of the other lads still in bed. Not having to but wanting to do it.

We were taunted by other kids, and it hurt sometimes but we carried on but while we worked together, we were ok. On Saturday the ritual of going down to Pakis and weighing in, were made up. We would wait until Sunday and with the help of Frannie Leonard (Chinney as we called him) we would climb over the wall of Pakis and pinch the scrap back only to weigh it in again the following week. Then we would climb over again and pinch the jam jars so as to break the cycle and not to let Paki get suspicious. Sometimes when weighing in rags, we would soak the rags or put bricks in between them to add weight. Sometimes we got away with it and sometimes we got caught.

Sometimes we would go out with my dad on a male family pub crawl. I've said before, how crafty my dad was! We would start off at Georgie Connors, then Billy Ditts, then The Smiths, The Delaneys, Eddie Carrs, the Lings then yeah! Yeah! And all my dad's mates – this is only in Gordy. In every house we would be given a tanner each and an apple and an orange. My dad's offer was a scotch or two in each house. From there it was up Everton Road, up Fairy Street or Havelock Street and sometimes Mittford Street, the on to York Terrace and on to my Aunty Annie's and Uncle Pats over Waterworth's shop. Up the entry my granddad lived so we would all get a tanner and some sweets and my Aunty Annie would give is some rhubarb and apply pie for my mam. About 11:30am before the pub opened, we would be on our way back home, the money was taken off us. Some went to my mam and we had the sweets and oranges and my dad ended up in The Gordon Arms, now you know where we got our craftiness from. God Bless him.

Chapter Three

Firewood and Football in that order

As you know from earlier in the book our main source of income as four young lads in and around Greaty was selling firewood. The collecting of firewood also has a tale to tell. Each afternoon from school on our way home for dinner we would collect wood. We would go to the bombed-out houses or empty houses. We would take off doors, skirting boards, architraves, window casings, floorboards etc. If it was wood it was gone. Anything that was wood and could be chopped up and we could sell. One of us would chop it up, normally me, while John and Alan would bring it in to the yard then one would start to bundle the wood. Then two of us would go back home for more while the other one or two if Ray was home would chop and bundle before we went back to school. So, at teatime we had a head start from others doing the same thing. Unfortunately, or in our case fortunately, they never had our energy, our guile or our determination to be one step ahead. It was about continuity and the customers knew who they could rely on and who would be there day in day out, week in week out, month in month out, year in year out, the Booths. We meticulously stuck to the script. If one of us was ill, the other three would carry the name forward. In the summer is wasn't as busy as not many people used the fires. Some elderly did and we knew who they were and they were not ignored. 100 customers or just 10 we were there keeping the established Booth name going. In the summer months w=there were other ways to make money. In the winter it was hard but profitable.

Our John and Alan would be sent out each night with 13 bundles of wood, held in front of them and I would tell them where to go. They used to call me all kinds of unprintables. But when we got there, we would start with Mrs Kinny, then Mr Gill, then up Gordy to Mrs Smith, then Mrs Gibson and Mrs Garr. From there we would go in to Elias Street then to Conny. Elias Street was always a tricky one. We had to be careful because we had Frankie hart who owned a wood yard producing bundles of firewood for the retail trade in chandlers, grocers and general stores, and corner shops. He never liked the idea we were in the street and often tried to make us leave. But we had ways of avoiding him and in the end I'm sure it didn't affect his business in the slightest. We never set out to ruin someone's livelihood, but it never helped. I am sure it did that there was another wood yard also at the bottom of Elias street, this man had only on leg. This would really tug at the heart strings. He was a good man but we carried on serving our loyal customer base which stretched to both sides of Greaty and our clientele were faithful.

Our customers ranged from old men and women living on their own to families. We were cheap and cheerful and fresh, you could trust us. We were reliable and we also gave larger bundles of wood, more than the bundles that they would have bought from the shops. From day one we tried to introduce them into the shops, but because of the crude way we had of chopping the wood by hand rather than machine, it was never in uniform shapes to go in to retail outlets. So, we carried on our door to door delivery service.

We were always polite, had change and never gave cheek. We were often given hot drinks in the winter when we were freezing, and we were so cold sometimes I would cry. I was tired and cold, but I wanted to carry on helping my mam. I hope and pray she saw the good in us. We worked hard, very hard, we were only kids. We had a purpose; it felt good to earn money at an early age without robbing someone's house or stealing or mugging an old person or breaking in to shops which some people did. What we were doing was giving a service especially to the old and the vulnerable, people who would otherwise be cold and of course they would be lonely and they knew we would call each night and they trusted us. We would talk and go for messages for them. We would help with demanding chore. We felt good. We had a social conscience. We were well behaved; no-one had a bad word to say about us. Most of the time we worked as four brothers. We never brought anyone in only Chinny. No-one penetrated 40 Gordon Street, the Aladdin's Den, only the scrap metal dealers through the tradesmen's entrance, the back door.

Gordon Street off Netherfield Road

Sometimes we had to resort to other ways of collecting wood. As we had been trading some years, most of the houses were still occupied and the others were stripped to skeletal proportions, so we had to wait until houses became vacant. So, we had to improvise and put out the net further. We would call at fruit shops, fish shops, local factories and builder's yards to obtain wood. We would go as far as the Dock Road, over Scottie Road, Heyworth street and Shaw street, Brunswick Road, wherever we could get wood to chop and sell, and remember then we had to carry it to 40 Gordon street, no mean task when you're only 9,10,11 and 12. We would ge3t our string from Sturlas, a local shop. We would strip each line from the coil making four lots rather than one. We never paid for string, ever. The fish boxes stunk and were tough, so we would mix the wood and put the fish wood in the middle, some would complain but we carried on selling firewood. We sold firewood until we had to leave 40 Gordon street for pastures new at 20 Luton Grove, Walton L4. I was 15, John 14, Alan 13 and ray was 12. We were mere boys but we shook the world before the Beatles.

Our other passion was football and street teams. We were all good and gifted in different ways. I was a good dribbler and was fast. If I pushed it past you, I was gone, you never caught me! I was a great runner and could beat most people. Our John was a great header for someone so small. He was also a great shot. Our Alan was strong, you never got past him and if you did, he would have you next time, especially at corners. You would be on the deck with a sore head. Our ray was always on the verge because of his age, he was four years younger than me. As we got older around 13-14 and ray was 11, that's when he started to get in to the street teams. As well as running the street teams, we arranged matches near and far as well as using my dad's silver chalice as a cup which we would play for. My dad picked it up somewhere when he was out with the barra. We played for that cup dozens of times. We lost it a few times by getting beaten, but we were back the next week to win it back. We were good and we would sometimes go as far as Everton Road to play street teams. We would go as far as Portland Gardens, Gerard gardens and Vauxhall gardens, all over Scottie. They were hard lads sometimes, sometimes there was bother, but mostly they were okay. We relied a lot on Franny Leonard. He always had a ball and we would have to let him play. We sometimes used one or two lads from the top of Gordy, as Gordy had four street teams.

When we had bomis there was always four in Gordy. One at the bottom, the Bothams, the Rogers and the Burns. Ours was just past the Gordy pub, The Benny Jones, Alan Rowan and at the top end there was

Eddie Carr, Jimmy Millington, there were plenty of lads to pick from. But there was always great rivalry and a few bullies, but you get that anywhere. Some were good, some were superb. But I must say our team could beat most. We never tired of playing football. We played in Penny School against the Hardacre's and the Melia's. Sometimes we would beat them, they were Catholics and we were protestants but we never had any trouble. Football was a great way of making new friends, some are still friends today. I was always on the verge of the school team, I was kept out by Harry Roberts, nicknamed Henge. He was good but I believed I was better, but not on the day because I scored 3 and he scored 4. We had great players. At school Billy Baker, he played for England boys and then went on to Liverpool. There was Ray Hoyle, John Marsden, and ray Lunt etc, I could never get in that team as they were good, never mind ... we all four lads had full lives so no time to dwell.

My mother at aged 18. Eat your heart out Elizabeth Taylor!

Chapter 4

Greaty and Our Schooldays

Greaty it had the lot during our school holidays. We would skip on the lorries. Up and down Greaty and there was the yellow mezzers, we would jump on the back, rip open the sacks and get out the nuts. Then there was the griddle, you could jump on the back and just sit there, they were quite slow. We got a good ride to the end of greaty; we would get off and walk back or skip on another lorry. One day I jumped on the back of Sturlas van just leaving Gordy. I was about 10 or 11, as it built up speed, I tried to jump off but it was going too fast. Once I reached Rose Vale I had to jump off. It was going so fast it scared me and as I jumped off, I rolled over and over and it was a dark winters night, about 5pm. I don't remember a thing, I was crying. There were women all around me and one woman said, "its Billy Booth's lad, wait till his mother gets hold of him". Anyway, the woman brought me home. All the cuts and bruises and my mother still battered me! You could do in those days. I can tell you I was more afraid of my mam than I was of my dad. We hardly saw my dad but my mam was ruthless. If she caught you, and she normally did, you would get the back of her hand and it hurt, honest to god it did.

Some of our great past times down Greaty were on a Sunday. We were playing pigeon toss and for money it was great. They had one man at the top and one at the bottom, playing dixie in case the coppers arrived and they usually did as that's why they were there. But you never knew how or in what guise they would arrive; a bread van, a delivery van, but never a police van, that came later. The men would scatter in all directions mostly down the back entries and the coppers would leg it after them and you could be having your Sunday dinner and someone would run through the living room and say, "Hiya Jane" and run out through the lobby and out the front door as though they loved there. You could be on the bog when someone would come in and say I won't be long. Have seen them hide in pigeon lofts and even in with the hens and chickens. They were not safe and a few got caught then the black Maria arrived, no need to disguise that van.

Anyway, me John Alan and Ray were quids in. As the men scarpered, we helped ourselves to the money and then we were off before we got caught. When my dad came in, he would ask how much did you get, knowing we would be there like vultures. We would say a couple of bob when it was really pounds. My mam would get most of it, and we normally gave me dad half a crown for his entrance fee that night.

Great Homer Street

Another good earner on Sundays was going down grids. We would start at one end of Greaty and work our way along. We would have a 608ft bamboo cane we bought from the chandlers on the Saturday and wed cover one end in chewy, gum or tar from the street. Then it was off down Cazeneu street end first. That is where the real money was made by the market on a Saturday. People would lose or drop money down the grids, especially the grids outside the pubs when they checked their money going in and out of the pub. We would lie on our stomachs, insert the sticks into the holes or grills and move the debris with the stick until something showed. It could be a tanner or a shilling but more likely it would be a half a penny. Mostly we struck gold. There were the three of us and sometimes we had Chinny with us. Two would start up one end of Greaty and two the other end and we would meet up in the middle. It was hard work and you needed good eyes but it was worth it – nothing passed us brothers. When you think of it there was a pub at every corner with a grid. We were ait it all day then at 4pm with our stomachs empty and our eyes and hands black we would meet and share our haul. It could be as much as six bob and if we were lucky £1 share that between four people about 4-5 bob (shillings) each after six hours on our stomachs. That is the equivalent of 20-25p by today's standards.

Can you see any kids today doing that for their sweet money during the week? Not likely, that's hard work.

The whole family except for Wayne and Gail who are 9-10 years younger than me went to school off Greaty. First there was Penrhyn School nicknamed Penny, then we went to Roscommon, nicknamed Rossi. Penrhyn school was a junior school. I first went there at 4. My man would take me and my teachers name was Mrs Rodgers. I remember the slide outside the class. I would play outside whilst my man went inside to talk about all the times, she had let me leave the class to go to the toilet but I ended up leaving school or climbing the railings or just walking out the reception class door to make my way home, always to be caught and brought back. I was a little escaper. I remember on one occasion my man had bought three pairs of leather or imitation leather trousers for me, John and Alan. I liked them, they were cool. But not in the summer! You sweated like mad in them. Anyway, one day I was caught short in class and when I eventually got to the toilet, I had shit myself! I went downstairs into the school yard and over the railings. I as about 8 at the time and small and the railings were about 6-8ft. I fell and got caught in the railings. I landed on my face and one of the railings cracked my front tooth. It stayed like that for 10 years! I ran home crying. I ran up the entry and into the house where my mam was with my auntie Letty. She went mad. "What's up, how did you get here"? "they stink, get them off"! My auntie Letty was laughing. I'm sure my man and dad did some laughing that day. We had many days like that.

In Penny we had our playtimes on the rood. It was great up there and when the ball went over it took ten minutes to get it back! Even at ten years of age there were some hard men. I remember Mr Biswall, our maths teacher. He called Tommy Farragher over to him to talk. Tommy ended up head butting Mr Biswall in the head and there was murder. I am sure he got expelled for that! Mr Biswall had a real crush on my man; every time she came to the school, he would eye her up and down. Even dressed plainly she had lovely skin, lovely eyes and a real Elizabeth Taylor look about her.

Roscommon Street School

While at Penny we would often go to night school. There was nothing much going on and it was mostly for girls. Mr Scurla who had the shop on the corner of Gordy paid for the school to be built. He was a good man and a great benefactor, when he was alive, he gave generously to charity and helped everyone to obtain a better education, paying for evening schools for the poor and underprivileged. From Penny we went to Roscommon or Rossi for short. It was a good school and we got more or less the same treatment there from the bullies or school snobs as we did at Penrhyn Street, the perpetual cliché "all right Boothie is your dad still a ragman"? well we put up with it, at first, it was me then the year after it was John then Alan and finally Ray for a short time. We left the area in 1963, Rossi was a great school, and the teachers were great too. We would play football in the backyard with Mr Barker, he was sound, he would give you work to do then go missing, god knows where! The football and the boxing teachers were great too. We had a few kids in Rossi who made it good in sport. There was my mate Billy Baker, he played school boy international and then played for Liverpool 'A' team. Then there was Harry Roberts, a good boxer. Mr Bossi and Mr Chisnall were hard, they had to be, they were in a hard area.

When we had PE in the bottom gym our John would bunk off school by going out of the gym through the window in the hall. A short drop in to the back of Roscommon Street; he would be off getting firewood, for the night as he would be off over the water with his mate, Billy Roberts, nickname Rabi. They would go to the outdoor fair in New Brighton and play the fruit machines and come home loaded. Mostly he would be looking for empty houses or one that was leaving that day. If we could all bunk school and get back before PE ended, we were ok. Mostly we got caught and ended up before the head.

A house was coming empty in Arkwright Street. Me, John and Alan went there at 12 o'clock one day we climbed over the backyard wall and proceeded to empty the house. We got all sorts, copper boilers, chairs, cutlery, mirrors, cables, brass fire surrounds, carpets. We made a dozen journeys through entries and no – one took any notice, it was common with the Booths. We were always moving something; second nature and I think people liked us for it. We were not leery, we were not cheeky and we were polite and industrious. We were brothers working to make our mam make ends meet.

Anyhow we stored everything in Aladdin's cave, 40 Gordon Street, tradesmen's entrance, the yard was chocker block. You could not move, this was a golden day. We were ready to value our days' work, we went back later to collect the rest. The next day at school Mr Botham, came on to the stage and said "would the boys who took the belongings from 22 Arkwright street please return them, they were not for disposal but to be moved to the lady's brothers house for his use. If the boys return the items of furniture nothing will come of it, if they don't it will become a police matter and I will deal with the boys myself". Enough said. Never-mind the police, Mr Botham was clinical with that stick and needless to say the goods went back. We never intended to take anyone's possessions, only if they had been discarded. Well you win some, you lose some. There was always tomorrow during those long summer days down Greaty.

Everton Heights – The Braddocks - 1959

Chapter 5

Roots and roles and reasons

As we were all from the Everton part of the area of Liverpool, that's where our heart was and also our family. It was a very close-knit community and those being born there were seldom moved from the area. For what we needed to do, Greaty and Netherfield Road was a big enough back yard if you like. We were very well known as a family and very well respected. Hard working lads through and through looking for the next money-making scheme, we never crossed the line. We were afraid of my mam, she had a wicked back hand. When she hit you, you knew about it. My dad just looked, that was enough. We respected them, we were no angels, far from it.

We could give and take, but mostly we knew which side our bread was buttered so we played the oracle, and we said yes Mam, no Mam and moved on. Our main aim was to keep moving, that was a saying of my dad's mate Cisco. He was a good laugh. He loved in New Street next to Bossi, where my dad was born. We had respect for the elderly and we never gave them cheek. All of the siblings had their duties and roles in life. As kids we played out well. I was the eldest and gave out the orders. It never always went down well, but we got results. I had an eye for business and we played on our charm. Don't get me wrong, John, Alan and Ray worked hard, sometimes too hard. We lost a lot of our youth, but we would not have missed it for the world. Our Alan and John were the gofers. I would send them on the furthest walks with a dozen bundles of firewood. It would be the depths of winter either pouring down with rain or freezing snow but off they went, my name was fit to burn. We had to make money each night, my Mam relied on it. When I look back, we were a great team. We all had different qualities. I was a schemer, I would always want to be in there first, always the element of surprise, waiting to nick the skip first. I worked year in, year out. Alan was strong, he was a nice lad and would do anything for anyone. But if you crossed him, look out! He would break your neck in one go. Alan and our John were close, always together. Our John looked quiet but he was not. He was hard, he would fight anyone and for his size was scared of no-one, but he had a heart of gold. Ray, four years younger, helped where he could. He had to be in early because he was only 10 and those days you only played under the lamp. We were a great team and we excelled in what we did. We had youth and energy, guile, cheek, enthusiasm, but most of all we had each-other which seems missing in today's kids. We had a purpose to get up in the morning, a reason for living. It was hard, very hard, and in the winter I cried. I did lots of times to myself when I was chopping wood in the yard, in winter, it went through you. But it had to be done, we made a rod for our own backs because we needed to help me mam. We were not playing with our mates who were comfortable in their world. Our day to day was set out in stone. We carried on doing what we started all those years ago when I was 10-11. It was a bind, we never let people down and we made it a bit easier for my mam and dad. I'm pleased to say we achieved the goal and in the end me, John, Alan and Ray did well. Job done.

Since those early days in Gordon Street, gathering all the knowledge we thought would help us through life's rocky road there has been great knocks and surprises, not least in the way we turned out. We re fresh eyed kids and our looks would get us the parish. Not anymore though. We still have the gift of the gab and could still sell ice to the eskimos.

After leaving school I got a job with Venmore's and ended up pushing a hand cart a bit like my dad really. It was chocker with building materials. My strength and energy kept me in good nick for £2.50 a week. From there I joined the merchant Navy and met Cathy my wife. I moved from job to job before we married and then went self-employed. When you are self-employed, the old charm and selling ability comes back and you carry on where you left off. My wife and I are still in business and now we are pensioners, with grown up children and grandchildren. Our days are still busy and apart from a few minor scares we are still in good health.

My wife, Cathy

Our Alan left school and went to work as a French polisher, served his time with Kennedys and then went to work on the railway. He had 7 children, 5 girls and 2 lads and several grandchildren. They are all gorgeous. He still works and has been with his lovely wife Sue for over 40 years. He still works hard, is still happy go lucky and as soft as a brush, just like when we were kids.

Our John died when he was young. It broke our hearts. He was generous, he was a scally, he was hard, he was quiet and he loved our first daughter Jane when she was a baby. She's 41 now. now. He worked at Grossfields mill, we all had a spell there. From there he went on the building sites and worked for Cubbitts and then he went in to the pub trade. He was a bar man and a cellar man. He was good and everyone wanted him. He worked nearly every pub in Walton. People wanted I'm to run their pubs while they went on holiday. He was honest and hard working. He had an eye for the girls, he had dozens. He was easy going and a soft touch when it came to lending people money. He helped them all, drunks, alcoholics and bums. He took no messing in the pubs though, he was hard. If he said "move it" you bet you were barred. Everyone was with him. He was number one barman. If there was trouble or they came back with a gang he had back up. They all stuck up for him and of course, they were his mate.

Our Alan, you never argued with big Al, he would kill you, he and John were always in trouble. They were like glue, always stuck together. When John died our Alan was devastated, he could not take it in. Ray was the same, and they all drank together each week. It was the nature of the job, the hours, the stay behinds, his drinking which to us was minimal, a few pints a day, was enough to kill him. He had no wife, no kids but plenty of girlfriens. He lived with my mam and dad and had the best of care. Three meals a day and his own room. He got in to a rut starting to stay out, not eating his meals, and he developed cirrhosis and he was dead before he reached his 50th birthday. My mam and dad were in turmoil, no parent wants to lose a child so young. He was well liked and got a full house and at the church and down the streets. He is still talked about today on Walton road, he was so popular, I still miss him every day. He will always be the bogey man, the Booth, the bogey, and the best darts player on Walton road, and the best bar man and gigolo. Miss you mate.

Chapter 6

Ambitions and different paths.

I have to say the person who surprised us all was our Ray. He never got to hold a hatchet because he was too young. He never got to use the oracle on the customers or duck and dive like us three had to and he was spared carrying firewood because of his size and age. He never got to pinch clothes off lines or lavatory seats to be painted and sold on. He never had to sell wood in the freezing winter nights, he was in front of the fire with my mam while me, Alan and John were out freezing to death for a few shillings. He never knew the rules to make money from all quarters. Yet he was the one in later life who would leave us all standing. He may have picked something up as a kid or was already in us all. Like my dad, who was the master of all of us, we were his apprentices. Our Ray has done well. He worked his way up and he knew what he wanted and he got it. Good luck to him. Because while on the way up people were trying to shoot him down. He had the oracle and he could use it, he made a good living and like us kids he took no prisoners. He capitalised on his education in the days of in reach of St Polycarp's.

I have to say as the eldest what life has dealt out, starting with my sister Gail. She is married to Brian and has one child Claire. Having worked for Boots as a Rimmel sales consultant for years, before and after Claire, she had been unlucky with her health, with constant back pain. She and Brian are happy and as I write, she will have her first grandchild in early 2012. Great news. Gail is turning 50 now and misses her soul mate, our mam. Ta-ra girl.

Now on to Ray, who was married to Carol they have been together since teenagers. They have a boy and a girl, Neil and Rachel. He has had a very successful and varied life and has achieved a great deal from our early years down Greaty. He is a successful business man and would like to think he inherited his guile and his success while watching and learning the art of the oracle. He has come a long way from out of our 2 up 2 down terrace of 40 Gordon Street. Good luck kid, the boss.

Now it's Wayne's turn. Unfortunately, he was only a baby when we were plying our trade down in Greaty. I am sure he would have made a great addition to our cause. Imagine 5 Booths, the customers would have been well taken care of. His looks alone would have been worth an extra few customers per day. Wayne and Mary have been married over 30 years, Sarah, Kevin and Marie. Unfortunately, Billy-Bob died as a child and as my name sake. It was a great sadness. Wayne and Mary have weathered many storms. Who knows if he would have carried on Wayne's many talents of his football and darts. We would all be drinking in the news bar by now with all the others. Wayne was too laid back for that type of life. Keep it up mate... 180!

Then there was John and then there wasn't. He was a real cad. He could charm the birds from the trees, mostly the female type. Imagine blond hair, blue eyes, who wouldn't say boo to a goose, until you crossed him. What a dart player and left handed as well. He could strip a length of copper wire in two seconds. Paki never knew what day it was when our John told Chinney to move it and get over Pakis wall and start passing the scrap iron back over. A true leader, generous to a fault. He helped all his mates and a few Judas. They could never match up to him. A pint of bitter kid, and don't forget me change mate!

Then of course there was big Al, 6ft odd and a heart of gold. He certainly had a social conscience. If he thought you were hurting, he wouldn't sleep that night. A real Robin Hood. He loved kids and would have made a good disciple. But then he might have been better had he not lost his minder. He's hard and you don't cross him. Him and John were joined at the hip. Little and large, what a combination. He would give you anything then ask for it back that same day. He married Sue and they have 5 girls and 2 lads and they have all turned out a credit to their parents. Stephen and young Alan are all taller than their dad. All the girls are beautiful women. They have 4 grandchildren and have been happily married for more than 40 years. Good on you mate, see you in the Dunnies, it's your round.

And finally, there is me. What can I say? Me and Kathy have been married almost 42 years. We've been together since we were teenagers. Where has it gone? We have 3 beautiful daughters. Obviously, they came from good looking stock. They're Jane, Suzie and Kate. We have 4 grand-daughters and two grandsons. One who is made after me, what an achievement. From someone who started his days up and down entries. The proverbial back entry didler. Kathy and I have been in Garston for almost 42 years and in business since August 1969. And I must say, if I went back all those years, I would still argue with may mate over her. She was lovely. We have had sad times and good times, but I do as I am told. We are ok. But I will leave you with this, those 4 kids ruled great Homer Street and even today, don't let my grey hair deceive you. The brain still ticks.

3 daughters: Kate, Jane and Suzie

Chapter 7

The growing years

After leaving school I always wanted to go away to sea, my dad went, his dad went, and so it goes on. I went to the Careers Information Office in North John Street for school leavers and there were literally loads of jobs. But I wanted to go to sea. I took a temporary job for 6-12 months in a building contractors, it was Venice Street off Robinson Street. The nature of the job was that myself and an oller man would get a work sheet, we may have two –three jobs that day. We would load the hand cart, that's right, déjà vu, the barrow returns. Anyway, once it was loaded with bricks, cement and mortar, slates, ladders etc we would be off. It could be Anfield, Everton or Walton or even as far as Kensington. I would push the barrow, just me, 5ft nothing and 7-8 stone dripping wet. There must have been 200 weight in that hand cart. My mate would walk alongside the cart holding on to the side, he would be on the side walk and me on the road. Needless to say, it would be me pushing the hand cart with all its weight while he merrily held on to the cart, with the other hand on his bike whistling a merry tune … usually, home on the range where the deer and the antelope play.

He was a great mate. When I got to know him. The job was hard and we walked miles and pushed that hand cart up Sleepers Hill and Everton Valley. Day in day out. The job only paid buttons, but I learnt a lot. The lads were great and the men who only earned a small wage helped us a lot. I took home £2 11s2d a week. My mum opened my wage packet and gave me back the 11s2d. I never needed much. I bought chewing gum, I was too young to drink and I never smoked. But I was partial to a 6-penny bet each day.

Our job was to repair any problems in the 200-300 properties our employer, Mr Venmore owned. And the jobs carried on from day to day. From replacing a washer, to climbing up a 3-storey ladder with a chimney pot on my shoulder. That's scary especially on Netherfield Road which slopes to the bottom. My mate was on the roof. I was on the ladder with no-one holding or footing the ladder and half a hundred weight on my back. No health and safety in those days but I managed to stay alive and after 12 months I applied to go away to sea training school. I passed my aptitude test and medical at the pool in Mann Island and was told I would be sent along with dozens of other boys aged 15-17 by train to sea training school on MV Vindikatrix in Sharpness, Gloucester, otherwise known locally as the

Vindi and to all the local people we were known as the no good Vindi boys, sent there to mend our way – not true!

Our 6-8 weeks in Sharpness was hard, very hard, it was freezing as it was Winter when I was there. The River Severn was frozen and our huts or billets had no heating. We were up at 5 am and on the parade ground and put through our paces for one hour in shorts. It was freezing and the start of a very long day. The offers, all ex seamen were fair but hard men. After early morning exercise we went back to our billets and we cleaned them from top to bottom for captain's inspection each day! If it was even slightly dirty and he had on white gloves we had to do it again and forfeit breakfast. If it was clean then we all went down to the ship, the Vindi, which was moored on the river Severn, parallel to the make shift toilets on the quay.

She was tied up, was about 60-80 years old and had had some history! She served as a training ship with classes and had a canteen and a galley for the boys, perfect on site along with the officers and staff 400-500 at any given time and breakfast was not fit for a dog. The porridge was cold and watered down, the scrambled eggs were inedible and the bread and jam were stale. Cockroaches would fall from the deck heads and the bulkheads. The sip was a breeding ground for insects and I'm sure we all left there a stone lighter. We all looked forward to the food parcels sent from home each week by our mothers or when the could afford them. It was an experience. We were taught seamanship and catering skills. Not all the boys wanted to cook. Some wanted to become wingers or wailers, as they were known. Nautically speaking I'm sure the 6-8 weeks we served there, the harsh weather, long days, bad food, as virtual babies mixing with strangers from all corners of England Ireland Scotland and wales, made us grow up quickly.

A view of Everton looking north from the top of the new flats in Conway Street, 1965

It's not what today's kids could do or even think of. Imagine taking their mobile phones off them! They would all fall over every five minutes. There was no health and safety like there is today in this liable society we live in. You were thrown in the deep end. You had to get a pass mark or you went home, not to sea. Remember those days. Your parents paid for you, you never got paid. My parents went without for me to go there. I could not let them down. I behaved myself, didn't get in to trouble, stayed with the scousers, got on with my work and the weeks went slowly by. We went off to camp at the weekends and we would go down to the docks and go to the seaman's mission. We would drink juice, play darts, table tennis, or eye up the local girls, which were few and far between. Remember they thought we were supposed to be on the vindi for rehab, not sea training. It was all rumours and lies but some of us gained respectability and we had the church on Sunday in Berkley which most of us attended. We went to the cinema on Saturday night, all innocent fun. Some boys climbed the fences at night and went AWOL. Some were sent home for getting in to trouble or for stealing. I could not do any of those things, my mama would have killed me. There was one girl who became an institution whilst we were there but she had a name and most of us kept away!

During our time there, I learnt later, that some famous people trained on the Vindi; Tommy Steele the singer, John Prescott Deputy Prime Minister. If you got through that training it would and did shape your life. No-one or anything would sway you after you left the Vindi. You could tell a Vindi boy later at sea and the camaraderie was great. Once a Vindi boy always a Vindi boy. I'm proud I went and I learnt a lot there. On leaving and in our final exams, I was not the brightest boy there, but I managed to finish with 86/100which was 3rd top of 40 boys in our class. Not bad for a lad from Greaty. I was made up and couldn't wait until my mam and dad found out.

When you look back you realise what a great form of discipline and self-respect that was instilled into every boy who left the Vindo. Remember when the Vindicatrix Sea Training School was opened it was so that boys as young as 14, 15 & 16 could be quickly trained and sent to sea, possible to be killed on their first trip to replenish those crews who were being torpedoed by the U boats whilst carrying goods, food etc in the Atlantic during the second world war. No matter what we said as boys about the Vindi it never applied when we reached adulthood.

After going to various reunions at the dockers club in Sharpness every August its surprising how time flies as most of us are close to retiring now. Retiring from work though, not life. Some stayed at sea, some only did one trip; the weather and the conditions made up your mind for you. Some moved away, to Tasmania, America, there were some millionaires, a Governor of New York, doctors, lawyers, entrepreneurs, entertainers, MP's and they all went to the Vindi.

The bond is fantastic but sadly now each year it becomes less and less as people pass on. Remember it was 64/65 when I left, it only lasted another 2 years after that. Those who went before me will be in their 70's, 80's and 90's. And it was harder in their day. But what kept the name going and the bond stringer was one man called Ray Durning. After leaving the navy, he was a fire officer and after returning from the fire service he made it his business to research the Vindi Boys past and present. They were as far afield as Tasmania, they came from different backgrounds but they came each year to the Vindi reunion. There are still hundreds left alive to tell how it was to be a Vindi boy. I'm very proud to be a Vind boy. To have lasted the course, to have attended reunions, early March each year in Sharpness and in hindsight, if they never scrapped the Vindicatrix back in the 60's what an attraction it would have been. Even today, without the Vindi, the hotels are full and the place is heaving. Ray Dearing was awarded the MBE for his drive and devotion in bringing together a part of this sea faring and sea training history and, I'm sure if it was not for him, I'm sure we would have all passed away un-noticed. I am proud to be a Vind boy who are known all over the world. The camp and the officers did a great job in shaping their trainees in to respectable and Disciplined young men. Power to the Vindi Boys!

Chapter 8

Bad Days, Good days, Home.

My trip to sea was not long after I left the Vindi. My dad was working on the docks and we moved to a new house in Luton Grove, Walton L4. It was a bog house compared to Gordon Street. They only built six in the road and there were 30 kids living in them, obviously built for a reason. Anyway, I had signed on to the MV Malatation, which was going on a six-week trip down the med calling at ports at Gibraltar, Piraeus in Greece, Beirut, Latakia Cyprus, Dublin then home. The chief Stewart and Stewart were called Gabby Martin and Bengi Cohen who were Spanish called at our house in a taxi to pick me up. I was only 16 and I was petrified. Not only was I going away for 6 weeks but there was a seaman's strike on and the ship was sailing. We arrived at the ship in Langdon Dock, boarded the ship and she was sailing on the next tide. I was told to stay in my cabin and lock the door – this I did! Whilst we were manoeuvring the ship from the dock you could hear the bricks and metal hitting the side of the ship. It was scary. We were getting called scabs and being threatened. I knew nothing of the strike. I was 16. Lost and scared. We were all shuffled in to the mess where I was to spend most of my days. We were given something to eat and we were all introduced to each other. It was not a big ship, 1000 tonne cargo boat. There was the skipper Mr Penkele 1st and 2nd officers, 2 cadet officers, a chief engineer, and 2nd engineer, 1 chef, 1 comis chef and a pantry boy (that was me!). 1st Steward Bengi Cohen and one chief Steward, 1 Bosun and 4 deck hands, approximately 20 people, but in a small ship we all had to get on. We were eventually told about eh strike, some of the senior men were not bothered.

After a few hours' sleep that's when it all began! My initiation. I was called at 5:30am, got dressed and went to the mess for a cup of tea. Then my duties began. Being the pantry and galley boy, my duties never stopped! I had to clean all the alleyways, the toilets, the bulkheads, the portholes, rooms belonging to the offers (not crew), I did this with Bengi the Steward then at 7:30 I had to assist the cook with preparing breakfast for 20 people. Once that was over, I had to clean the pots and pans and help Benni clean the dinning saloon after the captain and officers. Then I could have my own breakfast and this was all before 10 o'clock. Then it all started again, cleaning, bringing in stores form the pantry for lunch, peeling spuds, preparing vegetables, and all this on top of being as sick as a dog for two days. I was strapped to the sink for a whole day being sick. I would go on deck and peel spuds while the ship tossed and turned my stomach. I felt as though I just wanted to die. After two days it all calmed down and we entered calmer seas and cooler weather. Our first port of call was Piraeus, Greece. It was a Metropolis of broken-down ships. It was and still is one of the longest ports in the world for breaking up and scraping of ships. As we arrived there was the usual activity on the quay. Street seller; women with shanks on their shoulders trying to barter for goods, drink, cigs, mainly in exchange for sex, but we were soon moved on. Once we docked the rest of the crew set off for the bars and brothels. It was an eye opener. My first trip to sea and a brothel at 16. Well we won't go in to that. That was part of my initiation. It was a lovely City Piraeus and if we had been there longer, I would have liked to see the Acropolis in Athens. As a young boy I thought we would be back but we never were. We went everywhere else though! We rapidly moved from port to port. After Piraeus it was Beirut Latakia, Famagusta in Cyprus, Alexandria Egypt, Dublin and then eventually home. It was along 6 weeks.

But guess who was waiting on the dock for me when I arrived! Me mam. My dad was there too with his friend Tony Bennet. My dad had a bag with him. I realised what it was for soon enough… woodbines!! It was obvious. He came for the loot. Woodbines, roll your own tobacco, whisky, and a dropsy in that order. He was a case! He took some beating. There we were, the boss and his apprentice, just coming home from my first trip to sea. It was while I was away that the family had moved from Gordon Street to Luton Grove.

While I was on leave, I thought me and my mates should try and get in a pub. All my ex school pals used to go in the Oporto, bottom of Arkwright Street, but our John, Rabbi and his mates went there so I tried the Brown Cow next to Cazeneu Street market. It was good – we were in! 2 pints of brown mixed and we were pissed!

It was soon time to report back to the ship and this time we were heading for Jerusalem and all the Jewish ports. This was a short trip; only 3 weeks and after that I signed off. It was time for the big stuff… Harrison Lines, Shell and eventually passenger liners and Canadian Pacific.

It was on the Empress of Canada that I met up with an old friend, Cliffy Woodage from the Vindi; he was a bell boy. We used to have a great laugh. He was from Blackpool and used to get on great with the scousers. After the Vindi we had gone our separate ways but I met up with him in my Forties whilst I was working in Chorley for Securicor. He was married to a Maltese lady called Vicky and had two girls and a boy. We used to visit 2-3 times a year for a meal and a few drinks. I must say Vicky didn't like me taking Cliffy to the pub at dinner time. She used to say he can't hold his ale, he only needs three pints and he's gone! One day we went out and started on real ale, then he went on the scotch, he started on the manager, had a go at one of the regulars, came home and went to bed. An hour later he got up and thought the wardrobe was the toilet! It wasn't his wardrobe though, it was Vicky's! After that she never liked us going out. I still get a Christmas card; signed Cliffy, but no Vicky.

Brownside, 29 March 1967
The famous Rupert Dome (Everton FC symbol)

During my Seagoing years I did a fair amount of ravelling. I eventually left the merchant Navy and had a selection of jobs; Bibby's, Crossfield's, bonded warehouse and Frank F Scott. Whilst I was at Lamb and Watt bonded warehouse most of the days were clouded in a haze. All that sampling of cherry brandy! Most nights I couldn't navigate the cellar steps to go home. I had to get out of there. That job was killing me and I wasn't even 21. From there I went to Frank F Scott, shipping butcher. It was here that I met my first real girlfriend, Carol. She had short dark hair and was pretty. I had to get someone to ask her out for me as I was too shy in those days and not confident with girls. We went out for a date and I was with her for 9 months. She lived in Rock Ferry. She said it was over and I cried for hours. Being turned down hurt. She preferred Tom Jones to me. What the hell. Your route is mapped out for you and better things were to come.

After a dozen or so not so good jobs, catering, car wash, warehouses, our new neighbour Lilly Alexander worked facing the new houses we had moved in to in Luton Grove. She worked at the butter factory. She got me in and I liked it there, blending the butter with the boss called Don. He was a drinker. You could tell by his face that he liked the scotch. Anyway, I liked the job. It was across the road, I was working all week, going out of a night to my local pub, the Pacific and I was in the darts team, one of the lads. I had a few girls, I thought I was god's gift! One day I was invited by Lilly Alexander to go to a party in Shiel Road, Kensington. I went with my mate at the time Reggie Walker. That was a big mistake! We arrived at the pub and me and Reg were half cut. About half an hour later this beautiful girl walked in. long dark hair, mini skirt, what legs, what a body! She was the one who turned all the heads. She was gorgeous! At some point in the night I plucked up the courage and asked if she wanted a drink and she said yes. I bought her a brandy and Babycham. I was skint after that. After that we all went back to Carols house, a friend of Cathy's. I was in the front room trying to speak to or dance with Cathy. After a while I got to talk to her and dance with her. Reggie was not happy as he couldn't get a girl and he wanted to leave. He was drunk and kicked off and we got told to leave. I was fuming. I waited at the corner of the entry for Cathy to come down. She came down but we were not allowed to go back thanks to Reggie. Her friend thought we were fighting but we weren't! I arranged to meet her on the Sunday afternoon after she had been to church at St Robert Bellamines.

I was there at the corner by Orrell Park Ballroom. Guess who was with me... Reggie! I never thought she would come but she did. Her mum was with her. She asked what he was doing here. She said, "I'm not going out with the two of you!". At that point I said, "get lost Reg" and off we went to Carlton Picture house. Guess what was on? The Family Way! After the show we went to the Warbreck pub for a drink. Cathy had her usual Brandy and Babycham and I had a Guinness. I was never confident with women but we got through the night and I walked her home. Would you believe it I missed my last bus and never had enough for a taxi. I asked Cath could I borrow enough to get to Walton and she leant it to me. I was over the moon. She was beautiful. That was a good day!

Chapter 9

The Great Journey

After that date I never thought we would carry on together. She had a lot of friends, lots of male admirers. I really loved her and wanted it to work. Most of our courting was spent at the pictures or on days out. We had no car but we would go to Wales. Cathy loved to climb. We would get the bus from Birkenhead to Mold and spend the day walking. We never had any money. During the early years courting Cathy I was in and out of work. I could not settle after going away to sea. She used to pay for most things. We had our ups and downs but mostly we were happy. I was only interested in getting married. When we did, she started with our first daughter Jane. She's 42 at the time of writing this (2015). Doesn't time fly? Makes me feel old.

After we got married, we spent our honeymoon ...working! We got married in 1970 and Cathy opened her first hairdressing salon around the same time. She was 22 then and is still working in the same business and never stops. She takes after her dad, Wally. He was great. I got on well with him but he died young. Cathy is like in many ways, hardworking, eye for detail, loves anything to do with space, volcanoes, travel, weather shifts. A mind full of information, that's Cathy!

I was working on the buses from Walton depot during our early years and we were living in Garston which is where the hairdressers is. They were long days when we were young. I was not the easiest person to get along with. I have to say I drunk too much in those days and it took its toll on our marriage. Several jobs came and went and I was out of work for periods of time. It never helped when Cathy had to work to support us. After those dark days we managed to pull through and are still here, happy and I hope still in love after all these years. I look after her and vice versa.

After the first seven years Cathy carried on running the hairdressers and I opened up a newsagents in Wallasey. I used to get up at 3:30 each morning and drive to Wallasey to open up. I would sort he papers and the paperboy would arrive at 6am to deliver them. A local lady called May would arrive at 9 and work until 12 while I went the wholesalers. From 12 noon I would stay there until 8pm the drive back to Garston. That went on for 3 months and then me, Cathy, Jane, Suzie (who was born in 1974) all moved over to Wallasey where our third daughter Katie was born in 1977. It's funny really as even though we all moved back to Liverpool in 1979, all three girls have lived within touching distance of that newsagents in

Wallasey as adults. Katie even worked facing it at one point. Fate. It takes you on a journey. Really uncanny.

When we moved back, we lived above the hairdressers in Garston for a little while. Then Cathy spotted a house nearby and we bought it. It was a back to front house (kitchen at the front). We did a lot of work to it and after a few years we moved again, closer to where Cathy came from originally. We bought a lovely bungalow in Melling and we are still there. So, at the time of writing this we've been in the hairdressers for 40 plus years. We never thought we would stay so long. Cathy is a great hairdresser. The customers love her and she is a local institution.

We've had a few other hairdressers as well, they were called faces and were in Walton and Great Homer street. I managed them and after they closed, I did other jobs like Securicor and group 4. Our daughter Suzie opened a sunbed salon next to Cathy's hairdressers called Jermaine's (the name of her daughter and our first granddaughter). Suzie ran it for 2 years then went through a break up from Jermaine's dad so I took over the running of the shop. We've upgraded over the years, opened up another unit next to the sunbeds and we are still here and still working.

Cath and I have come full circle. We should finish and do all the things you're supposed to like travel and have time off but why tempt fate? I am still healthy and I look after Cath and we get by. We see the grandchildren every week and I hope we have brought up three intelligent, hard-working, responsible, grounded, caring and humble girls. When we set out together all those years ago, we never thought we would still be here, doing what we are doing but life has a way of dictating your pace and path. Suzie became ill while living in Scotland with Jermaine. Thankfully she came through it and eventually moved back home after being up there almost ten years. She works hard. Katie has three girls Caitlin, Chloe and Evie and is married to Barry. Barry is hardworking, laid back and loves his family. Kate is like Cathy, hardworking and loves a laugh. Jane was married for years, living and working in London and Yorkshire. After 13 years she divorced and went on to have children with another partner. She has a degree in History and has two sons, Will and Reuben.

I think me and Cathy have come a long way. The road hasn't always been easy. It's been paved with robbers and jealous people who were envious of what we had worked so hard to achieve. 16-hour days and one day off a week for almost 50 years. We brought up three children, nursed sick parents, were on committees for this and that and latterly haven't been blessed with great health but I'll tell you one thing, no one female can follow Cathy. She is so strong inside.

I have been blessed with inspirational women in my life; my nan, my mam, Cathy and our three girls. I have been a lucky man. I went down one entry as a young boy and came out a man. I've loved it and would do it all again. It's been a great journey and it's not over yet!

Signed W.H. Booth
"The Boss"

Mam & Dad and brothers at Ray's house party

A Compilation of short poems and assorted photographs

A History of thoughts put in to words

1.   In goes your eye out
2.   Annex of my mind
3.   Tomorrows kids
4.   Just a little bit of me
5.   This is a tall story
6.   Just like one of the Jones's
7.   Voyage not complete V.N.C. National
8.   I used to be unemployed but I'm alright now
9.   The docker's have gone ta ra ta ra
10.   I know it's alright because Kilroy told me
11.   Kids
12.   Move over while I die
13.   Let me be me
14.   The valley of no tomorrow
15.   Shanks
16.   Dedicated to Ivy and Harold Norris – content in the knowledge

In goes your eye out

You walk outside, you take your share
You think it's all worthwhile
A sigh of hope, a sigh of joy
A sigh of grief and sorrow
A life today and death tonight
Who knows who says tomorrow

When this old world
It gets you down
There's not much left to say
Just drink your drink
And eat your jam
And die from day to day

My Auntie Letty ad my Nan

Annex of my mind

If you think there is an answer
To the problems of today
Well the overall response
Is to turn and walk away

So if you like helping
But you wish to shield your views
Then join the rank and file
In another of the queues

Kathy's of Garston shops and flats complex

Tomorrow's Kids

It's not the beginning for others who have none
Just another tomorrow for those who have some
It's expressed in their salary and in the toys they buy their kids
Like up and coming Fauntleroy
With Clarkes shoes on their feet

Pakis Scrapyard

Just a little bit of me

One pound fifty pence a pint of bitter
Two pound for a smoke
Don't you think it's stupid
Or is it just a joke

As you know a fiver's nothing
I mean to have a good night out
If I went out with £2.50
It's only short and sweet
Soon we will abandon morals
And stay inside and let the kids go out

My Nan on her way to Gordon Street

This is a tall story

If you believe in Jack and Jill
And a little Jackanory
In life I believe in war and peace
Now there's a short story

I used to think that men were men
And women worked in kitchens
But that was once upon a time
When people told tall stories

St Polycarps

Just like one of the Jones's

If anybody came to your door
Say no more, say no more
Send them on their way, on their way
Don't let them know what went on today
Hide it, hide it

Keep yourself to yourself, to yourself
Don't tell the world
You are by yourself, alone
Just like some of the Jones's
Like one of the Jones's

Old Nessey Road

Voyage not completed V.N.C. National

I was only a boy when I first went to sea
But I prayed for that day for so long
After fifteen years in a house full of kids
My calling was soon very strong

I remember quite well, my very first days
As they grew longer and longer
As the weather became worse
As my heart beat stronger
As the ship became bolder and bolder

As it tossed to and fro
Like my old toy yo-yo
And soon me and my ship were parted
But I was ok, in a life boat that day
And the voyage was over before started

Church and Conway Heights

I know it's alright because Kilroy told me

I have seen it in the kitchens
In the bog and on the walls
At the bottom of the stairs
By the fire where I crawled

In the dustbin, by the bus stop
In the betting shop on the door
But the best place I saw the slogan
Was down my local dole
Written in capital letters
KILROY WAS HERE AND IS STILL HERE

The Gordon Arms

Kids

Inside there is no salvation
From time to time
No way of remaining worthwhile
No hope, no salvation
No tears no joy
Just a word called the past
When I was the boy

I envy their faces
All covered in dirt
The way that they laugh
When others get hurt
The food in their stomachs
Some good and some bad
As I cling to the memories
Of when I was a lad

The Valley of Tomorrow

2,000 men worked down that mine
It was all they ever knew
But to everyone else
The view that they held
That all them down there
Were indestructible

But to the miners' surprise
And everyone's eyes
Their future never looked so good
The mines they were old
And the ceilings were cold
And the water was coming in fast

Then up went the sign
At twenty past nine
Were sorry to say
That the mine has had its day
And there's no money left to secure

So from that day forth the village was empty
Only trams and vagrants about
Well so much for the future
When there aint none about

The Shanks

When Shankly came towards the kop
He touched our very hearts
He never came in a flash fur coat
Or smoking a big cigar
He came across as one of us
Whose philosophy was simple

And so to what was once the fame
The Kopites had at their feet
All that's left is the memory
Of the man whose voice was warm
Would make your heart tingle
But no more will his shadow fall
Amidst the ground we used to mingle

So come on all you Scousers
Let's hold our heads up high
And think about those glory days
When Shankly left his native Scotland
To be an honorary Scouser Och Aye

Bill Shankley. Manager. Liverpool F.C. 1958-1974

Content in the knowledge
Dedicated to Ivy and Harold Norris

It only seems like yesterday
When we were face to face
And memories keep flooding back
At such a pleasing pace
And every day I think of you
I know that this will be
A common part of all my days
That keeps you close to me

As the days go by and weeks turn into years
The memory of your smile alleviates the fears
And yet I feel less troubled now
I know you are safe
And I as well as you my Harold
Have that smile upon my face

Appendix   Word reference to meaning:

Oller	waste ground or open space
Bomdi	bombed out house after the air raids in the war
Barrow	handcart
Fade	bruised fruit
Tarmac	area used for football matches
Tatter	rag and bone man
Weighed in	term used for weighing in scrap metal for cash
Bossy	Bostock Street
Gordy	Gordon Street
Greaty	Great Homer Street
Bomi	Bonfire
Chinni	Franny Lennard
Homer	Picture House
Lorry	Motor vehicle
Yellow Mezzer	Mill Lorry
Griddle	Mill Wagon
Weighed in	another term for paid or collected
Coppers	police
Entry	alleygate between houses
Tanner/sixpence	two and a half pence in today's money
Skip	to jump on lorry or wagon
Mary Ellen's	barrow ladies
Loosie	single cigarette
Leg it	to run after
Penny	Penrhyn Street School
Don't crack on	don't tell
Nessi	Netherfield Road
Dixie	look out
Lobby	hallway
Entrance fee	few bob to get in a pub
Bunk off	escape, get out
Rabbi	Bill Roberts nickname
Bunk in	get in for free

Back Roscommon Street

My brother John (middle)

John, me and Alan

My Nan

Daughter Jane and grandchildren Reuben, and Will

Jane, Will and Reuben

Cathy, Jane and Me

Cathy, Jane and Me at Jane's University Graduation Day

Daughter Sue and granddaughter Jermaine, who the business is named after (Jermaines One)

Daughter Suzie at Aintree races

Barry, Kate and Sue

Granddaughter Evie, counting pebbles at home

My granddaughters Chloe and Caitlin partying

Jermaine and Boyfriend Mick

My sister Gail, neice Clare and great niece Poppy-Jane

Jane, Kate, Sue and Myself

Evie Aged 5

Cathy and me at the Captain's table aboard the Appollo

Cathy, Me and Lady Scarisbrook

Appollo, at which we sat at the Captain's table

Captains Table aboard the Appollo

Cathy and me at a BBC function

Me and Cathy in Marbella

Me and Cathy

Receiving an award from Tom

Me, Cathy and 3 year Old Jasuka

Our business premises, Garston

Office and Reception at Jermaines One

Printed in Great Britain
by Amazon

51085254R00048